Free Verse Editions
Edited by Jon Thompson

Also by Elizabeth Jacobson

Poetry

Not into the Blossoms and Not into the Air

Her Knees Pulled In

Are the Children Make Believe? (chapbook)

A Brown Stone (chapbook)

~ ~ ~

Compendium

Everything Feels Recent When You're Far Away
(Poetry and Art from Santa Fe Youth During the Pandemic)

There Are as Many Songs in the World as Branches of Coral

Elizabeth Jacobson

Parlor Press
Anderson, South Carolina
www.parlorpress.com

Parlor Press LLC, Anderson, South Carolina, 29621

© 2025 by Parlor Press
Printed in the United States of America
S A N: 2 5 4 - 8 8 7 9

Library of Congress Cataloging-in-Publication Data on File

978-1-64317-495-2 (paperback)
978-1-64317-496-9 (pdf)
978-1-64317-497-6 (ePub)

1 2 3 4 5

Cover image: "Sea Goddess" © 2023 by Alexandra Eldridge,
   alexandraeldridge.com. Used by permission.
Book design by David Blakesley.

Parlor Press, LLC is an independent publisher of scholarly and trade titles in
print and multimedia formats. This book is available in paperback and ebook
formats from Parlor Press on the World Wide Web at https://www.parlorpress.
com or through online and brick-and-mortar bookstores. For submission
information or to find out about Parlor Press publications, write to Parlor
Press, 3015 Brackenberry Drive, Anderson, South Carolina, 29621, or email
editor@parlorpress.com.

For Marcello Vita Modigliani,

*In this morning's sunshine
an illuminated face sings.*

— Ikkyu

Contents

There Are as Many Songs in the
World as Branches of Coral

A student asks:
What is the sword so sharp that a feather blown against it cuts away delusion?

Baling answers:

Each Branch of Coral Holds Up the Moon

The Yolngu people of Australia envision our moon
Filling with ocean water like breath coursing into a body,

Then washing out again. This is their theory of tides.
And just as each branch of coral upholds the glow from our moon,

Everything touches everything else, no matter where
Any one thing or any billions of things exist in the span

Of space and time; yet no things become two.
This is our essential nature, revealed

By the hair-splitting blade of the sharpest sword
As it conjures distinction.

There are as many songs in the world as branches of coral:
Each one a glorious, brutal dream.

I

Rhapsodies

Quantum Foam

The air is close by the sea and the glow from the pink moon
drapes low over a tamarind tree.

We hold hands, walk across a road rushing with traffic
to an abandoned building site on the bay, look out across the dark marina.

Sea cows sleep by the side of a splintered dock, a cluster of them
under the shallow water,

their wide backs covered in algae like mounds of bleached coral.

Every few minutes one floats up for air,
then drifts back down to the bottom,

without fully waking.
They will do this for hours, and for a while we try to match

our breath to theirs, and with each other's.

In the morning, sitting in the garden beneath thatch palms,
we drink black coffee from white ceramic cups.

Lizards killed by feral cats are scattered on the footpath.
I sweep them into a pile with the ones from the night before.

Waves of heat rise from the asphalt,
and we sense a transparent gray fuzz lightly covering everything

as if there were no such thing as empty space,
that even a jar void of substance holds emptiness as if it were full.

Love, I Am

All day *this thought*
had me reeling—
did not vanish
and then return—

was persistent
like a ceiling
leak pinging into tin.
Opaque rain all day—

what am I
to myself:
two feet on
some land

when upright;
a backbone with branches
when supine? Thoughts
become

weary—
and merely announce
linearity. Love,
I am

so wary of this
happiness, when
it floods in—when
it tumbles to a halt

—a rough cut ruby
at the center of a silver bowl.
Rain is the loneliest color
then lake, then shade.

Canyon Road

Driving on black ice
I brake too hard—
spin into a 360

and then two more.
Like the boom of a sailboat,
the back of the car

slams a dog.
In the midnight darkness
I get out to find a coyote,

his abdomen torn open.
The canine holds my gaze
as I cradle his head,

one palm above his brow
the other on his snout,
and hug him to my thigh,

until the chasm
of his breath closes.
An aloneness

not loneliness
comes from the animal—
yellow flecks inside his eyes

flash for an instant
before they turn to ice. I carefully
tuck the coyote's cooling body

under pine brush, rest my fingers
on his forehead, cover him with snow.
Nothing is made less by dying.

Walking the next morning,
in the early fog,
I watch a Cooper's hawk

fly up and up above the road
to scan the world for prey,
then spiral down, effortlessly,

as if it were a single feather—
hollow shaft travelling
toward white frost.

Notes on Desire

Archytas of Tarentum said the most fatal curse
given to men by nature is sexual desire
which fills the mind,
displacing more important thoughts.
Like what's for dinner
or what's happening at the stadium
in downtown Tarentum?

There are eight of us in the room talking about desire.
One person says, *I always want what I already have.*
Another asks, *Is there a want that has no yearning?*
A third chuckles, *No "I," no problem.*

Desire is the boldest gift of all.
A pair of burying beetles
sanitize a mouse carcass with their saliva,
mate on top of it.
When the offspring hatch
this is what they feed them.

A female mockingbird calls *Chip chip*
And the male responds *Chip chip awwwwwWWW,*
his deep throated trill at the end
gets her to move deeper into the powder puff leaves.
Chip chip chip chip chip chip, she says.
Gator, gator, gator, gator, gator, he says,
and flies to her tree with a twig in his mouth,
jumps on her back and wiggles his tail.
She cranes her neck, tries to shake him off.

Best to keep hitting yourself on the head,
is what an ancient master said,
as he slapped his student in the face
with the sole of his shoe.
The mockingbirds are still in their tree.
I can overhear them.
Build me a nest, she says. *Make it soft.*
I know you, he says. *It will never be soft enough.*

Shooting Star and Bolide

One came from the east—

faint as a strand of long silver hair.

A few minutes later—the other—from the north—

brilliant like the blaze of a rocket.

Lying there on my bench, my back cold against stone

I felt welcomed by space

and the isolation it conjures.

Then this darkness, which courses over everything

turned greenish—then gold—then translucent.

Socrates said a soul, in its departure

from the body, will be dispersed

and driven away by the winds,

and be nowhere and nothing

in another world—

but I am still here, with mountains all around me,

a body to be alone in—

a consciousness that is next to nothing,

and full of the cosmos.

The Sweetness off Each Other's Bodies

Although October days are still hot, I harvest the winter squash,
buttercup and turban not growing any fuller

on their shriveling, waxy vines.
The ropy umbilicus is easy to cut,

so I finish the work quickly, take my clothes off,
make a pillow of my shirt and lie down

in the high desert meadow of browning yellow gamma.
A few blue flax still bloom

among the Mexican hats and blanket flowers whose colors bleed
maroon to red to orange to gold, as if washed in warm water.

Above, bees and June bugs swarm.
Each one lit with its own current,

which follows the insect like a contrail.
Yesterday I gathered the honeybees in my gloved hands,

dropped them into jars,
and dusted them with powdered sugar to kill the mites.

The bees become ecstatic when released,
eat the sweetness off each other's bodies.

Before dusk I walk into the nature conserve,
take my seat on the bench above the pond.

All autumn I've watched two beavers gorge on water lilies.
Their front paws move like trowels,

as they scoop the plants quickly into their mouths.
The smaller one looks up from eating,

keeps its eyes on the larger one swimming closer
and tips its face slightly out of the water.

Through my binoculars
I watch their anticipation, then I see their mouths meet.

They press their lips together, and hold them there.

Not One; Not Two

The foothills thrive with wild daisies and the warm soapy smell of Apache plume. A red ant with a missing back leg pushes a tip of dry grass three times its size along the dirt trail, arriving at a small branch where it cannot push the parcel further. I lift the branch, and the ant resumes its task. I pass an enormous anthill teeming with movement. Someone has placed a plastic straw in an opening and the ants tunnel out, landing in a heap on top of each other. In the windy canyon below, a pair of white throated swifts mate mid-air. Their eggs will hatch in a nest of twigs and moss glued to a rocky cliff with their saliva, which ants will climb to lick. On the patio yesterday, I watched a burly carpenter ant get trapped in a web a spider was actively weaving, then work its way out to attack the spider. The insects wrestled on the concrete until the ant had the final swipe and marched off, leaving the spider stunned. An hour later, on my return through the foothills there is the same red ant with the same piece of dried grass heading toward one of the openings in the big mound. Several from its colony hurry to meet it, and from this ant, two workers take the grass tip, carry it in front of their heads into the nest, while others investigate with their antennae, the space of the ant's missing leg.

For Whom Do You Bathe and Make Yourself Beautiful?

A black widow tends two webs in different corners of my bathroom.

She crawls back and forth on the white plaster wall

between her traps,

eats from the abdomen of a millipede first,

head of a pill bug next.

A male widow doesn't spin a web.

He destroys a female's snare so other males are not attracted to her

and sacrifices himself after an involved courtship

in which he gently binds her legs with his silk.

After my bath, water dripping on the floor,

the widow crawls from a nook, rests her carapace over a droplet.

Black widows don't need to drink water;

they get ample fluids from their prey.

With the flashlight on my phone beamed at her head

I see her palps moving, flicking droplets onto her body,

shaking them off.

No House

after and for Gerald Stern

Before sleep, we listen to a podcast of Jerry reading his poem,
then I conjure the Erechtheion,
where on the north side stand six draped Ionic maidens
along a porch on which I have never stood,
and you dream about Squirrel Hill,
Reva feeding you raisin kugel at her ebony table,
the green Depression glass bowl and crystal dish
arranged on a lace doily.
We wake and what has changed
is everything—
an olive tree grows in the kitchen
and love is finally flooding into all the bombed-out cities,
supple and fossilized.
Our world was fashioned from gases soiled
with the residue of previous stars,
so we build with stone and cement,
pretend a temple,
but no house can hold us safe.
Ancient Greeks exercised naked with javelins,
wouldn't eat beans because legumes
contain the spirits of the dead.
They diluted wine with water to show refined behavior.
They built their houses around courtyards
the way a body is designed around a soul.
On the recording, Jerry's voice is sturdy and unclouded.
I see him carrying the colorful rugs of his body,
rolled and under his arms,
from one room into the next—
up the steps of green mountains—which rise through his ceiling,
then out the back door he marches,
carefully down stone stairs, into the Delaware river valley,
his legs a few short paces
behind the thrilling leaps of his mind.

Wasn't It Yesterday That Our House Was Full of Poppies

Our city river has fluctuating currents. It travels past our porch,
Down from the mountains, through the old part of town.
No one harvests the watercress growing on its banks. Not even the fawns.
Under narrowleaf cottonwoods,
Violet-green swallows nest in the willows, their young drop from high onto the broadest sunflowers
My husband plays his cello by an open terrace door.
Our children have grown and gone away.
Wasn't it yesterday that the house was full of poppies?
Baskets and baskets of them gathered from fields above our home:
What is the lure of this world? It is only the place where you let go of your body and the tenors of
Your life.

Your Life.
What is the lure of this world? Is it the place where you let go of your body and the tenors of—
Baskets and baskets of them gathered from fields above our home:
Wasn't it yesterday that the house was full of poppies?
Our children have grown and gone away.
My husband plays his cello by an open terrace door.
Violet-green swallows nest in the willows, their young drop from high onto the broadest sunflower
Under narrowleaf cottonwoods.
No one harvests the watercress growing on its banks. Not even the fawns.
Down from the mountains, through the old part of town—
Our city river has fluctuating currents, and it travels past our porch.

Ars Poetica with Pine Roots

Can I know what I am?   I am a host for many.

Do I know why I make these things?   This morning

    the desert air smelled of pine roots

spreading their ballads into the earth.   Expect

there will be a sunrise over steaming mountains.

Expect there will be   no reason

to empty what fills and fills—   to spend whole days

after whole days   sliding words around on paper—

to eat   one bitter blackberry   then another

from the same wild bush   and the eighth one is sweet.   Each

long exhale unwinds a confession.   Each footslog into the far

coniferwoods.   Paradise.

Moonrise over Hernandez

The baby never slept, and if she did
it was only for ten minutes at a time.
She wasn't distressed, simply inquisitive.
She didn't want to miss out on anything.

At dusk I walked her in my arms around the plaza.
The moon rising above Picacho Peak pleased her, the star
over Loretto Chapel, illuminating the narrow streets of town.

We climbed the softly worn stairs of the museum,
the uneven wooden floors giving way
under my feet like a well-watered lawn.
She craned her head and stretched her arms
toward the dark vigas of the ceiling with its
carved red and blue bulleted pattern.

In a narrow room painted the green of a young ponderosa,
she gazed at the Ansel Adams photographs,
moved her eyes across the southwestern sky of his prints,
pointing to the small white speck in the black sky
rising over snow-capped mountains, the river village of Hernandez,
and said her first word, *Up.*

Holding Hands Is Like Holding the Whole Body

Ice hangs off the roof like a bear claw.
Single drops of defrosted water
melt down long icicles which you catch
in a cup and drink with quick
licks of your tongue, pretending the taste of sugar.
You say: holding hands is like holding the whole body,
and you touch each one of my fingers,
naming it a leg or an arm.
You give each nail a part of my face.
I watch your small face at night,
green in the glow of the night-light.
It never stops moving.
Even the faint hairs on your forehead
seem to breathe as you dream you are
racing toward a gate swinging open.
In the morning you are up first,
going through the drawers in your bathroom
for a cloth to cover the doll house.
You rush into my room with your old baby bath towel,
the one with the turquoise trim,
and the little Carter's bow.
You say you remember this bow.
You remember that you used to try to pull it off,
that you wanted to tell me that you wanted to pull it off,
but you couldn't because you didn't have the words.
There is snow melting on the window frame behind you.
Drops fill the tiny squares of the screen
magnifying what's beyond into oblivion.
I cannot see past you. It is you who delivered
solitude's ending.

Fair Trade

My son shows me how to optimize the flavor
while making a cup of pour-over coffee.
He tells me to grind the beans
just seconds before the water boils,
any sooner, he says, may destroy
the taste. We watch the granules of coffee
packed tight into the unbleached filter
gurgle and drown in their crowded sphere
as he slowly drizzles water along the edge of the cone.
Fields of white jasmine-scented flowers
bloom prolifically on tropical coffee plantations,
each once a seed from the center
of the flower's ovary like my son,
who came from the center of me,
pushed up and up and then shot out
to be someone something else will yank apart.
Everything I teach him about caring for himself
doesn't seem useful, because what I should say
is that the first rule of nature is things deteriorate
before they get a chance to become whole.
A budding flower withers as it peaks
and exactly what's right with the world
is exactly what's wrong with the world:
bright red coffee beans are cultivated,
harvested, processed, shipped across oceans,
roasted, packaged, sold again then again
to end up in my kitchen, ground to bits,
waking me more fully each morning
while I sit on the porch with the old brindled dog,
who ignores our resident magpie
as it drops from the top of the high wall,
gracefully like a leaf, onto the dog's tired neck
and takes a tug at a scab on the top of his head.

One Taste

The Buddha said the ocean has one taste, salt, but I taste the green

alaria of the Atlantic, ropy and dense—I unwind it from the

tentacles of blue bubbles we've named man o' war—and suck its

silky tendrils. I taste the *eternal note of sadness* from the spray off the

cliffs at Dover Beach, the skin of those I am swimming with, and

those who are now back on shore—whale sperm, sea star arms, fan

corals, barracuda piss. The essence of the deepest dwelling

radiolarian, with their intricate snowflake skeletons, rests like a song

on my tongue. I open my mouth to the sea and in floods the flavor

of Albertus Seba's seven-headed serpent, with its slick emerald

prehistoric back and fairy tale humps. I taste a radiance from the

moon, always overhead, where dust smells like spent gunpowder. I

taste the way the black sand looked from the window of the bus

going down the west coast of Peru, an exhausted sea on one side of

the road, Shining Path shacks disintegrating into the pale dunes on

the other. I take the water in and swish it around my mouth, toss it

back and gargle with a throat full of zooplankton and single cell

organism-size bits of plastic hitching a ride in the cascade. I taste the

whale rise, their lime green fecal plumes at the surface of the sea.

Rich in nutrients, they feed the phytoplankton, which bob in the surf like invisible friends. I taste an oil slick of sunscreen, dark globs of sticky tar, metallic treasure chests of sunken gold and jewels, harmful algae blooms, feces from cruise ships. I smell the dwindling Colorado River water vanishing into human forms. I taste the burning retch caused by two fingers down the back of a throat, a thick coating on the tongue, the tang of scum and fetid water tormenting its own esophagus. I taste the smell of blazing old growth ponderosas aflame in forests too parched to resist a spark of lightning. Our screaming bougainvillea, our ornamental grass, our fields of corn, our poisonous syrups. There is an island in the North Pacific where albatross roost and die, their decomposing bodies reveal the colorful tangle and web of petrocarbon refuse. The Buddha said that just as the oceans have one taste, so in our lives there is one taste, freedom, but I taste a saccharinity, the stink of enchainment: all of us heaving the same tragic sea inside, a continuous wave after wave of what happens happens over and over. From the shore, the moon ascends pink above the Atlantic. How indifferent a sea feels with its suggestion of infinity. After a Leonid shower on a moonless night, I find moon jelly after moon jelly tossed from the surf, high on the beach. Wanting nothing more

of water their clover-shaped insides have turned fuchsia in death,

leaving the outline of a crown at the top of their translucence.

Bleeding Slowly to Death

Our world is laid bare on this dock by the sea
spread with hundreds of shark fins

cut from the living, heaved
out of

then back into
the deep.

When I was young, I believed

I could swim far out beyond the shore in safety,
if all the sharks were dead.

Hour of Lead

When you are by the sea on an island made mostly of cement

When in the morning there are no mourning doves susurrating
    in the strangler figs

No grackles raucously settling down in palm crowns at nightfall

When a brown anole fans its red dewlap
    defending its territory of pavers

And another crawls out from under a pile of moldering
    Brazilian Beauty Leaf leaves,

A greasy black tail sprout growing from its broken stub

When a cormorant dives for young snook in the bay then comes up
    empty-beaked, trembles on a rusty culvert
        to spread and dry its accordion wings

Where the mangrove forest is no longer a forest
    no longer an oyster grove,
        your raft no longer banked in its dense cabled roots

Because some days you feel incremental disaster in each second,
    which inflames the mind like grit in an eye

Because on these days, you are like a tongue cut from a mouth

Because on these days you know you will never be empty enough

You lie on the hot brick patio and sweat, your weighty limbs soften
    into the sinking mortar

You stare and stare at a blistering sky

When finally, having reached the very bottom,
    that place where self-absorption is flawless

There springs a wondrous moment, like a trap that has unhinged:

And you feel a slight coil of return—a slight lifting

Which you recognize as your species' uncanny ability
    to imagine buoyancy,
        where there isn't any,

As if this will cure one failure of the self after another.

For Valentine's Day, My Teenagers Make Red Sauce

With carrots and beets, because their mother avoids nightshades, how they
curl my fingers into fists and sweat me awake at 3AM,

how meticulously they have chopped parsley and basil, minced a few cloves
of garlic, piled them on small plates

on the cherry wood counter,
but the kids forget to cook the tubers, and the plastic beaker cracks,

the blender spurting red all over the white cabinets, the kitchen now
a crime scene of root vegetables, like the winter morning

they squirted a bottle of ketchup on fresh snow,
then lay on their backs making angels.

The Day after My Twenty-Seven-Year-Old Daughter Was Not Incinerated in an Apartment Full of Natural Gas, I Roam and Recollect

Stiltsville

My body is slumber.   And mirage

follows mirage.   The mind   bashes
itself,

though blameless.

A steaming cup of coffee on the granite counter

appears as if a hallucination.

I drive to Key Biscayne.

A mile from the small island's coast,

ten feet above the sea,
houses are perched

on rotting pilings—

a distant village in the open water.

Not many on the beach.   A pair of crocodiles

swim just off the shore
taking the waves,

their long snouts raised to the sun.

Sacred Valley

So green and aura-filled,
is what I remember.

We dined with other families at the inn
            on roasted lamb and blue potatoes
                        from the caretaker's farm.

Then a night of violent food poisoning seized
                        my twelve-year-old girl.

            With fists full of soft bread,
        she hiked the next day with us to Machu Picchu.

                    Her black eyes, her small hands,
            hugged the narrow trail
                        as she bowed under the firmament
                and burst

                        into clouds.

The Story of Her Arrival

It has to be one of the gloomiest human characteristics
to wish for something from the past
to return again: so when my girl calls
and says she wants her first room back,
the one that gurgled and swayed, suspending her
in that gravity-free chamber of my body
I say *deal with it baby.*
I'm out in the garden, with bees from the honey hive:
drones who are male, inseminate the queen then drop dead,
a queen who stores the sperm for her lifetime,
and the workers who are all female.
These bees don't mate like other insects,
not like the grasshoppers on the stucco wall the other morning
the big on top of the small, legs
wrapping and unwrapping around thoraxes
bodies shaking—not shaking—then shaking again.
These creatures were at it for hours, believe me,
I kept going to check;
so when my girl says she wants back in
I tell her to go get laid.
MOM! She cries, her big brown heart of a face on FaceTime,
a mysterious blend of Ashkenazi and Sephardic,
her black eyes stone fruit, the endless night sky of her dark hair—
all that making of her, days into evenings—
my legs wrapping and un-wrapping,
then over my head, propped up a wall.
It's her 24th birthday and she wants the story of her arrival,
the cave I hiked to the afternoon before,
the mucus plug the following morning,
the salmon I baked in the toaster oven
when contractions were five minutes apart,
believing it would strengthen me during labor
when all it did was cause me to burp salmon for ten hours.
Honey, I ask, *can we talk later? I need to get back to the garden.*
Bumble bees are sonicating in the sunflowers, vibrating like crazy–
their pollen baskets are brimming.
As long as there is desire, honey, you will suffer.
But without it, you flat line.
And I hang up.

I Don't See Anything at the End of It

—Larry Levis

Maybe you heard about the clever kids
who wanted more views on YouTube?
They thought an encyclopedia would stop a bullet
from a handgun, so the 19-year-old girl, pregnant
with her second child, shot her boyfriend from a foot away
while someone filmed. Maybe you read about how elephants
can understand human pointing. How each elephant
in the study goes first to the trainer's hand
which points to a bucket of apples, then nuzzles
the fingers with the soft-lipped tip of its trunk
before moving on to eat the fruit. Maybe I've mentioned
I go weekly to the men's shelter on Alarid street
where we read and write poems around an orange
Formica dining table. Yesterday when we read Larry Levis'
Boy in Video Arcade one of the men jumped up with a wide grin
and said, "*SHIT, MAN!* What happened to poetry?"
Maybe I told you how David and I were hugging in the kitchen while the
coffee was brewing, the dog was standing there,
looking at us, a little clear stuff dripping from his nose,
when suddenly he opened his mouth and out flew
a butter-yellow Cloudless Sulphur.
Maybe you have studied bird languages.
I am learning magpie.
Their favorite word is *Mine.*

Very Long Marriage with Lacerations

One of you has slit a finger while opening a parcel
with the Exacto knife kept by the front door
while the other is hanging up a coat,
tossing keys in a basket. There is blood
on one of your thighs. One of you
takes this bleeding finger into your mouth
while one of you puts the parcel down—
the one who wants to be in love with someone
else, while at the same time in love with what you are,
together, in the marriage—
wants both loves because silence in a backyard
covered with snow can be silent in the same way
a bay gleaming with the reflection of sun
is silent. And the children, born long ago now,
born into blood and shit soaked sheets, a room
streaming with light and elation, the children both
know the long silences of your marriage, heard one
of you wanting to destroy the other, watched
one of you put on your coat and not come back
for over a month. Startled, one of you wakes
in a hospital bed following a minor procedure,
and after looking around the room finds the other,
and this one, who has just woken up, looks
at the other as if the other was the one just waking
up after a minor procedure, and one of you falls
open upon the other on the propped-up steel bed
frame, equally exhausted and equally vital, like long-
stemmed tulips in a wide white glass vase, violet
heads spilling.

II

Lullaby

A Brown Stone

I knew she was dying without knowing what dying was. My head peeking around the doorframe, holding onto the sleeve of my four-year-old brother. White translucent face, white cotton terry one-piece with feet, the baby's droopy body in the arms of the soft spoken, rosy-cheeked nurse. Beehive hair pressed with an iron, white pants and shirt, white ruffled collar, pressed with an iron.

Always milk dripping from the corner of her curved, faintly smiling mouth, as if it were melted snow still holding its white color. Always the same crooked smile, always the same corner with the milk, always the head not lifting, hanging off to the side like a sock doll.

There was a continuous whir from the families surrounding our house. A lawn mower motor, basketball thuds, kids squealing under a sprinkler or a hand-held hose. Wet cut green grass smell of warm autumn, each family with its own car noises—revvings and screechings. A new sister who couldn't swallow. Neighbors calling to each other out of open windows to ones already in cars—cars packed with kids, kids sitting on the laps of other kids, front and back, eight kids in the white Opel going one mile to school, one mother driving, still in her nightgown, car coat not buttoned, maybe a breast would be flapping, showing a kind of white.

I never heard anyone say, *we don't know what will happen.* No one ever asked, *how is the baby?*

All the mothers were young but they looked old to us. Pointed fingernails polished red in the spring, red in the winter. Tight pants and flowered shifts and cigarettes with lipstick marks. Hair that curled up at the ends in one big continuous upside-down wave. I stole my brother's coins. Tricked him by trading the bigger nickel for the smaller dime. Five pennies for only one quarter. He was happy to end up with more. Everything else was so thin, like the constant stream of formula milk from the baby's mouth, her small pretty face never changed expression, never cried. A snow baby with black pebble eyes, held up by the rosy-faced nurse who slept in her room. We sat on the edge of the twin bed and she would put her in our arms, first my brother and then me. We didn't know the word trust, didn't know there was anything else.

The nurse held the back of the baby's head up, tried to get the milk to stay in. Her long fingers were velvety, slightly blue underneath. I would touch them while I stroked the baby's silk hair.

That winter there was so much snow we built an igloo in the front yard, just like the igloo in the polar bear book, with a square entrance we could crawl into. So much fresh snow came down we could hardly see each other's faces if we were outside the igloo. Sheets and sheets of it hung in the chill. Inside the igloo we made a wooden matchstick fire, sucked the melted water out of our mittens, sculpted furniture to sit on—ice benches and an ice bed with an ice nightstand. We brought in small branches from the pine outside and pressed them to the wall for decoration. We went into the big house for supplies: white bread, yellow cheese, purple jelly, mugs and plates, the Candy Land game.

More and more snow came down like heavy cream. Neighborhood cars in their driveways like igloos, piles of snow on the street like igloos. There was ghostly white daylight and then there wasn't. Streetlights came on. We jabbed a hole in the roof for the smoke to escape.

Two Shadows, a beam, the silence and the hum. Two waxing moons side-by-side, sucking the melted water out of our mittens. They never called us in, even after it was dark.

This was the baby's only winter. We brought her a cup of fresh snow, made a miniature snowball and placed it in her mouth which couldn't hold anything. On her dresser was a silver brush and comb set, a frosted porcelain candy cottage nightlight, a set of sixteen clay trolls with pink faces and stocking caps, tumbling and rolling and holding a ball—things the baby would never do.

This was a time when people didn't understand the feelings of animals, didn't think animals had feelings. Maybe also the feelings of babies. Especially babies who couldn't eat, babies who were shriveling instead of growing. *How could a creature have feelings if it couldn't think?* Without a thought insects were crushed, smooshed. Slugs covered in salt turned to green slime. A cat run over by a car at the end of another street remained there for days while the neighborhood kids poked it with a stick, tried to see what was inside. The red blood turned blue then brown then black. The matted fur stuck to the curb like tar.

All the mothers and fathers seemed to know what would happen, kept it a secret from the kids. I never heard anyone say, *I don't know, what do you think?*

When I woke up in the morning, if I listened carefully, a small voice told me what to do. Get dressed, go downstairs, eat cereal from a colorful box. Kiss the baby on her head. Pile into the Opel with the other kids and pay attention to the teacher. Brown-bagged lunches with crushed sandwiches, yellow and black cans of Mott's apple juice. Red leather car seats smooth like the palm of a dry hand. Flap pouches on the inside of the car door filled with toys and bright hard candies. The small voice said I should ask before I keep one. The small voice told me not to put one in my pocket.

Even ordinary days were neon, glowing. I never saw anyone not want more and more of anything that might float up.

2
Shame

Every girl has her troubles. Some are born misshapen. I was born with a tiny beating heart on the inside of my thigh. My mother had to take me to the doctor. I heard *Teratoma*. I heard *Venous*. I heard *Inoperable*. The doctor told my mother it would never go away on its own. Every night my mother applied a yellow cream from a metal tube with the end of a Q-tip. The dense skin burned and sizzled slightly, dissolving the extra heart week by week into a gluey dough. Other doctors wanted to look at the girl with the outside heart, wanted to see it dissolving, wanted to jab it with a silver pick. On days like these there was a bottle of chocolate milk in the leaden milk box by the kitchen door. One tall glass bottle filled with creamy brown liquid among three or four white ones. The milkman wore a white suit, a white cap with a black visor. He carried the milk from his truck on the street to the house in a metal basket. There were no doors on his truck, and he hopped in and out so quickly it seemed as if the truck never stopped moving.

My mother often had a cold while she was pregnant with the baby. She always wore an orange tent dress with a dark green collar. My mother didn't like to touch my heart. Sometimes it would burn and bleed. Sometimes it would leak oily pus, and I couldn't do anything about it. The small voice told me not to put the cream in my mouth. The small voice told me not to put the cream on my younger brother. I was in nursery school when she was pregnant and sometimes they made me take a van back and forth. The van driver drove fast. He had long dirty fingernails that curled into the steering wheel.

At first a warm stream of blood seeped out onto the stoop where I sat waiting for the van to take me home. It burned and frightened me, and then more leaked from the outside heart, more than had ever come out before, until my corduroy pants were so stiff I could hardly step up into the van. The smell was strong. The van driver knew. The other kids knew. I was terrified to move, terrified to get out of the van. Some of the blood rolled down my pant leg and onto the slate path as I walked to the house. When my mother bent to open the front door the pocket of her orange dress caught in the handle. The pocket was trimmed in dark green. The pocket tore open. I heard, *What is going on?* I heard, *How did this happen?* My mother spanked my bottom, which was cold and sodden like a drowned creature gone limp.

Frost covered the front lawn and crunched underfoot. It was a cold spring. In the morning I was sick to my stomach. I was shivering so violently my teeth clacked together. They told me that I had to go to school. They told me that I would have to go in the van from now on. *Both ways, back and forth, in the van.*

My dread was so grave I could hardly step into the van. The driver didn't say hello. The other kids moved away from me. At school I played with wooden blocks by myself in a corner. The bathroom was full of paint supplies, easels, rags, jars of dried tempera paint. I went in every few minutes to check if there was blood.

I never heard, *Take a deep breath and let the morning air fill your lungs.* I never heard, *For you the dogwood tree is blooming.*

3
Cement

When the baby was born she didn't make a sound, not then, not ever. *The baby was pretty, but dumb. The baby couldn't swallow.* This is what I heard them say into the powder blue Princess phone that hung on the wall in the kitchen: *The baby always has to have someone with her. The baby has beautiful dark hair, and a lot of it.* My brother and I stood by the side of our mother's bed and held her hand. She slept on and on while our father was at work.

At kindergarten we made a big circle. I put my right foot in, took my right foot out, put my left foot in and shook it all about. There were circles all the time, on the chalkboard filled with groups of words. *A* words like apple and ant and arm. *B* words like boy and bat and ball. There were circles on the floor for sitting cross-legged and playing hand-slapping games, knee-slapping games. Our teacher played circles and circles of songs for us. While we were singing, *I Want To Hold Your Hand,* I looked around the circle and saw Ronald Tetter's penis showing in his baggy shorts. That week his mother called to invite me to his birthday party. She told my mother that I would be the only girl there. Every day Ronald Tetter's penis found its way out of his pants like a worm crawling from the center of an apple after it had been cut in half. The small voice said look at his penis. The small voice said don't look at his penis. I could look or not look at him, and still I saw a penis, raw and pale and bald like a newborn mouse. One black eye swollen shut in the jelly-like pink skin. My mother said I didn't have to go to the party. She got out of bed and walked into the bathroom, shutting the door behind her. I could hear the water running while she was coughing, trying to get something up from her throat.

The air got clear and chilly. The smell changed from green to smolder. Red and yellow leaves began to fall off the trees and turn orange, then brown. The older kids on the block raked them into piles, and we huddled into mounds as they heaped more and more on top of us, holding still under the dusty piles, playing dead.

I asked my parents if they would play the Beatles for us, but they didn't answer. I loved *love love me do you know I love you*. I started to pick little holes in my brother's clothes with my teeth, sometimes while we lay next to each other on the den floor watching TV, other times I would go into his room and bite something that was hanging in his closet. We had eggs almost every night for dinner, with fried bologna. My mother scrambled them in a black skillet while my brother and I watched from the white Formica table. We had a big square electric aluminum omelet cooker and sometimes she would use this. She cut fluffy cubes and put them on our plates with a spoonful of runny grape jelly.

The kindergarten teacher had a meeting with my mother. They sat on little red chairs at one of the little round tables while I played on the other side of the room with the puzzles. My mother wore her orange tent dress with the dark green trim, a bulky matching green cardigan. She said her stomach still hurt from the baby who was already 11 months old. The teacher told her that most afternoons, after school is over, after all the other kids have gone home, she finds me still waiting on the front steps for someone to pick me up. The teacher said I told her that I liked to watch the janitor sweep the sidewalk. The teacher said she saw me nibbling pieces of the cracked cement.

4
Wound

I spent hours and hours, day after day, wandering in the woods at the end of my street. Tall tree woods full of oak and maple and sycamore, trees that gave up their leaves to a permanent collage covering the damp floor of the earth. I loved the way my sneakered feet sank down into this muddy canvas. The thick brown glue of each dissolving season was dense and cushioned, always moist, and seeped up to coat the bottom white rubber edge of my Keds. A shadowy smell encased me as I roamed. I felt as if I was in a dream inside a giant acorn shell, wondering all the time about where the baby went. *The baby fell asleep. The baby never woke up. The baby is in the clouds now.*

In the spring, soft purple heads of skunk cabbage poked out of the gooey earth by the brook. I loved to push my fingers through the yielding part at the top, the foul smell pouring out like an infection. But now the plants had withered and their odor had flattened into the soil as its end was also its beginning. This world seemed seamless as I drifted. Young sycamores bent toward me and opened their arms. Lying down at the base of a massive oak, in front of an opening in the trunk like a small cave, a perfect diorama of a cave, where something warm could get in, like a chipmunk or a squirrel, and make a home, I saw withered roots hanging down from the top like long slender fingers, felt them caress my back as I tucked in. There was an animal curled up inside my tall little girl body like an embryo in a specimen jar floating in formaldehyde, but coming alive, stirring, inch by inch—a caterpillar becoming a moth—something confident and untaught.

As a child in a childhood, days seeped on like strangers. They were creaturely, sensory. They flowed back and forth, around and around, without boundaries, without shape. The small voice said who took the baby away? Did sleep come and wrap her up and carry her off in a bundle, or did death do this? The small voice said, will you be taken away like the baby, will your brother?

Sounds from the cul-de-sacs that made up the neighborhood bounced in and out of the woods like the echo of thunder. I licked and licked and sucked the skin just under my lower lip. It was constantly chapped, red and flaky with bloody cracks and bumps. I pulled the soft caps off green acorns, fitting them to each of my fingertips, opening and closing my hands, each finger a puppet with a hat. I split the acorns and picked out some of the bitter yellow meat, eating the rest like a squirrel with the scraping front of my teeth. I examined a plain brown stone that was even on one side and jagged on the other. The baby was there one night, and the next morning she was gone. The rosy-faced nurse with the soft blue fingertips was gone. Her twin bed was made and covered with the black and white checked bedspread. All the baby's clothes and blankets were gone. The baby's crib had been folded flat, and it leaned against a wall in the baby's room.

I picked at the skin around the sides of my nails. Picked and picked until they were open and bleeding. I sucked the blood from the cuts and the soapy taste made my stomach ache. Maybe in a dream the baby could hear herself talking, could eat, could swallow, could float after the scent of food, swim in the air toward the voices of her family. My kindergarten teacher taught us a lullaby. Told us to sing it at night after the light was turned off. *Now I lay me down to sleep, I pray the earth my soul to keep, if I die before I wake, I pray the earth my soul to take.* I didn't know what a soul was. But I thought that it might be something that puts out feelers, like an ant. I tapped on the inside of the tree to see if anything would tap back. I tapped again. I pressed the side of my face into a pillow of damp leaves, and chewed on the sweet tasting skin around one of my nail beds. Maybe the baby followed a dream into death or death into a dream. The small voice said, pick up the brown stone. The small voice said, it is the story of who you are.

III

Devotionals

There Are as Many Songs in the World as Branches of Coral

I walk a long way
sinking in soft sand.

My feet, two creatures
of burden.

Low lying clouds
mirror stormy ocean waves

and wild eddies.
The wrack line

littered with elkhorn
with coral sponges—

each one a finger
from a different hand.

Disappeared
are the reefs

they arose from.
As a child

I combed black rocks of a jetty
prying starfish from pools

sucked salt
off their legs,

curious podia searching
my tongue.

I craved also
the taste of ash

ate cigarette butts
from the beach—

put anything in my mouth
to know it.

.

I was nine
when I first saw the photographs—

bodies overflowing
from wheelbarrows.

Corpses pitched
in heaps like firewood

at the sides of barracks.
Didn't recognize what they were.

Then I noticed the bird,
a raven,

eating the inside
of a human nose.

.

There are as many songs in the world
as branches of coral.

The sponges
the sea pens,

the whips,
have a bloody

earthy smell.
I lay the few I've collected

on a wicker table to dry
under the adonidia palms

and squeeze out the remaining brine.
Soon they begin to sigh.

.

These hours
when the sky is white

my heart reels
like a cay in a squall

and I arrive again
at the scowl

of the red brick gate.
There were no clouds

that day, above the camp.
The grassy fields

bright green.
Tall birches

in full leaf.
I walked weightlessly

on the train tracks,
one foot

in front of the other
balancing on rails.

I pulled a rusty hair pin
from the soil

put it in my mouth—
Seventy-five-year-old tarnish

a perfumed
female essence.

The remaining brick
chimneys crumbling,

splintered garrisons—
burial pits moaned—

here was an endless landscape
of hatred this primeval—

it was as if I saw
each soul

who had arrived and
departed,

shimmering,
impossibly,

in the emerald fields.
And everything

broke open
and sang.

.

There were no clouds
that day

I visited Birkenau,
but the sky,

it was white.
The meadows,

they glistened,
the tall birches,

beckoned.
Before I left

I ate a few blades of grass—
peeled off a strip of bark

pressed two sharp stones
into my well-made shoe.

Three Stages of Friendship and Grief

1.

ABRAXANE® (albumin-bound paclitaxel), Gemzar®
(gemcitabine), 5-FU (fluorouracil), ONIVYDE®
(irinotecan liposome injection)

I was wondering if your eyelashes had fallen out
when you emailed this morning
to tell me when you woke
they were on your cheeks,
and on your pillows.
Fine little piles of butterfly kisses
for the fiends who race around in your body,
with their fast balls
and beloved game of hang, draw and quarter.
A delicate pile of commas,
that when brushed off
began to squirm like the legs of pale spiders
accidently broken from their bodies.
You wrote how you licked the tips of your fingers,
pressed them to the eyelashes now fallen
to your chest, and blew them
out your open window into the devilish spring wind.
Looking toward the Ortiz Mountains
at the gold mine in the distance,
you realized the sandy place,
just under the highest peak,
wasn't sand at all,
but an abandoned exploration site
where the trees had not yet reclaimed
what was theirs to make wild again.

2.

Square Watermelons

At my house all the female spiders are running around
with egg sacs on their backs and all the males have been eaten—

their insides drained as if with a straw.

My friend emails: *My arms are getting skinnier and skinnier.*
Not something I want. Really.

In Japan they grow watermelons in boxes to achieve
identical square fruit, which stacks easily.

Actuality and absurdity—two containers, one lid.

My friend emails: *We must accept the disorganization of consciousness*
as the natural fact.

This makes utter sense to me now—not measuring.

When listening to thunder, I email back,
most people don't know that what they are hearing is the shape of the landscape.

3.

Elegy with Birdhouses

In just a few hours each autumn all the gold leaves
drop off the mulberry tree

like a brief, heavy snowfall, and land in drifts
at the base of the trunk.

Grief moves this way—lyric in its enthusiasm to settle beneath.

The cadmium yellow birdhouse, sits slightly lopsided
in the branches of my tree,

its round portal black as a scream, its slanted roof
piled now with snow

will soon have tiny icicles hanging from the eaves.
You left other birdhouses

painted hot pink—painted a blue pale as cold lips—
in lanky aspens

growing by the banks of an arroyo where neighbors walk.
Some say you sing

solitary in the late afternoon, sounding like the mockingbird
that sounds like a killdeer, calling

untroubled
into the softening rime.

Mother's Day with Birdbath and Wildfires

Her pale reddish breast is so full
I gather it is being pushed up by the eggs
she is about to lay. I watch her dip and scoop water,
using the lower part of her beak like a gourd.
Her tongue flicks as she tips her head back
to send the clean liquid down.
She repeats this eighteen times
before she catches me in the window,
flits off. In the dailiness, a false dusk
descends. Dust to— and the flourishing
that is arriving moment by moment:
I have already had my coffee, chugged
two glasses of water, FaceTimed with my kids,
eaten a few of the dark chocolates they sent,
the third load of laundry is spinning;
I've moved geraniums from their winter
resting place in the house to outside under the porch,
cut dead branches from a limber pine.
I strive to make everything impeccable,
as it disappears. Our sky is dystopic gray,
abundant with ash, the patio covered with it, the open
cups of yellow tulips full of cinder.
Do I actually smell the ozone disintegrating—
its metallic scent permeating our air? Naturally
there is a connection between the twelve fires raging
in all directions around my Southwestern city and our car
that caught fire, burned up with ten others
on a shipping trailer on I-20, Kaufman County, Texas.
Like everything that burns to a finish,
it turned dead black. Charred dead
along with four hundred thousand acres
of Rocky Mountain pines, junipers and cedars of the Jemez,
ponderosas of the Sangre de Christos—
the deer, the elk, the rabbits, the coyotes, the flies,
the wolves, the raccoons, the marmots, the mice, the moles,
the rats, the lizards, the snakes, the butterflies, the spiders,
the worms, the skinks, the skunks, the bears and all the birds

who could not fly, their wings singed,
their eyes dried to dust bowls.
And what of their flesh—how will it reappear?
The robin lands on a ground feeder, lifts a mealworm,
then another, hops out of sight searching in tall grass,
when suddenly she flies up into the cherry tree
with a beakful of my hair
that earlier I pulled from my brush
and released in the wind.

Everyday Order of Backyard Creatures

For thirty minutes I stand at the bathroom window
and watch a fat squirrel devour one crab apple after another.
The rust and purple fruit look festive hanging like holiday
ornaments on branches bare of leaves for weeks.
As the squirrel leans her ample body across the crook of a bough,
reaches for the next piece of fruit, her hind legs
splay as far as they can stretch, and she inches backward
to dig the long shiny nails of her feet into tender branches.
Swiftly, she eats this crab apple,
then releases her forearms from a thick limb,
flipping acrobatically, her body relaxing like a hammock,
as she drops down to pierce one more small apple with her mouth.
The fruit rotates deftly in her paws, is eaten in a frenzy.
The undesirable core falls to the ground.
I have a clear view of her private openings,
the eight black nipples protruding from her tan underfur.
A pair of finches who have been watching from an adjacent pine,
dart to join her, pecking at the tart apples,
not so much out of necessity, it seems, but rather in imitation
of a good idea.
The squirrel's black acorn-shaped eyes,
circled in pure white fur
as if thin rings of makeup have been applied,
don't wince with the finches' activity,
or when a magpie swoops in, knocking a finch out of the way;
but when she turns and sees me in the window,
stares hard in my eyes as if she grasps how to look at a person,
she flees, taking her entourage with her,
and I stand there,
language swirling around in my head, a chaos
of enchantment and refusal.

Coronae

Four times before nightfall, a hummingbird visits the empty crown
feeder that sways from a beam under the porch. There is no sugar
in the house and striped grey moths leave halos of blood-red
droppings on the edges of window screens, on silk curtains,
on my pillow while I sleep. They are powdery and tough to catch.
I trap one between my fingers, shove a door open for release
as it wets my hand with a pungent pheromone that won't wash off.
From my room, I watch online as men in Florida throw dollar bills
out the sunroof of a car, crowds hazardously spooling
and scrambling. A few days later, George Floyd's final words float
on a banner through the New York sky. O is a thin-ringed empty
planet. O is a nimbus of torture around a bubble of grief.
White ranunculus open in glazed green planters
where I pressed the bulbs down into moist potting soil
a few months ago. A late forcing for an early spring bloom,
the flowers start as balled fists then unfurl in a ceremonious
burst revealing coronae velvet as midnight void of moon. The shape
of the circle never lets you out.

Other

Another friend is dying. She has a cancer that preys on Jews. She is full of tumors and the medication is not working. Jews are susceptible to certain types of genetic diseases like Tay-Sachs and Gaucher Disease and Retinitis Pigmentosa and Maple Syrup Urine Disease, which as a result of a missing enzyme produces toxic substances that build up in a body, causing urine to smell like the golden nectar. Jews are ten times more likely than others to have a BRCA gene mutation which increases the threat for breast and ovarian cancer. Some women I know with this mutation have had those body parts removed after their children were born. My friend who is dying had a friend who died several years ago at 68, and the two of them have the same name. The deceased Ruth, when alive, was furious and could not accept that she was dying. My friend Ruth shared with me the frequent complaints of others who were trying to comfort and care for the dying Ruth. I remember saying that if I was dying at 68 I would be angry, too. My friend Ruth just *hmmmmed*, and we joked that, really, the fiercest Jewish gene is worry. Together, we talked about all things Jewish and organized a discussion group for Jewish women. One of the topics was when faced with a question of race on a medical form, we were never sure what to select. African, Asian, Caucasian, First Nations. We were none of these. Even my progressive Jewish doctor did not have the appropriate selection for me on her form. We all said "Other" is what we usually checked. Ruth was hysterically laughing—she was chewing and laughing and she accidently spit some of her food across the table while she said, *Some of us appear white because our ancestors were raped by the Cossacks!* When I googled race online I found these same four categories and a comment that stated, "The concept of race is separate from the concept of Hispanic origin", which is confusing as Jews are usually categorized as Sephardic (from North Africa, Middle East or Spain) and Ashkenazi (from Central or Eastern Europe). My research also yielded that the Caucasian race includes Aryans, Hamites, Semites, which is contrary if you consider Nazis. However, according to the book *Caste,* there is no such thing as race; the term is merely a concept. Humans are all the same species with no strong genetic distinction. During the pandemic years my friend Ruth and I fell out of touch. At first, when I rang her, she seemed nervous, even over the phone, and stopped reciprocating. Was I being spurned? Later I heard that she was going out, seeing many other friends, waving her middle finger at the virus. It was well over a year that Ruth and I had not communicated when I learned she was dying. Many years earlier, when it seemed a mutual friend of ours might die almost instantly from bile duct cancer, Ruth and I were frenzied, phoning and emailing, trying to figure out how this could have happened. It was my first experience with a friend my own age facing nothing but deadly options, desperate to stay alive as long as his body could hold up. This was a person whose mind would never desert. And then it had to. Ruth and I were panic-stricken—what would we decide, faced with these circumstances? We agreed that we did not think we could take the poisons. It is unbearable to imagine into another's life, unbearable, I imagine, to fathom what it is to live in your own when it is coming to an end. After I knew that Ruth was dying, I emailed her and she wrote back. She said it was nice to hear from me, that she had a fast-moving cancer, that she was not going out, and that she was sorry to have to share this news. I am very good at perseveration, very good at saying I am sorry, over and over again, very good at envisioning the worst. I heard today from a friend that Ruth is centered. I am not sure what this means: Ruth twirling at the center of our planet. Ruth teetering at the center of a circle. Ruth warming her hands with her favorite coffee cup, sitting at the center of her kitchen table.

Dear Middle Age,

How did that young woman walking in front of me
with the red velour hot pants, her long legs travelling up
and out of view, how did she know
to buy herself flowers and carry them home in the fold of her arm—
to poise at the street corner just so,
hair glistening?
And did I know these things?
And if I did, why don't I know them anymore?
Earlier I rode my bike carefully around the new track
in the public park,
under rows of towering royal palms and stadium lights.
The ¼ mile loop surrounds a new AstroTurf soccer field,
its canned paint color reflects the blaring South Beach sun
as if it was the recollection of sunlight.
Some boys were running sprints.
You could tell which kids were really trying—
eyes pressed wide open, grunting.
When they were done the coach yelled,
Today you youngsters taught yourselves how to go
as slow as possible.
Over the long weeks, when they were pulling up the cracked asphalt
and real grass,
people hung out of windows across the street
smoking cigars or weed, surveilling the workmen,
and breathing in the plastic fumes.
I watched when they poured the orange liquid
that gelled into a spongy new track.
For months the smell was horrendous,
and that's all you talked about
to a neighbor on the street, when you greeted.

Ephemera

Even though it is dead
there is a vibration radiating

from the grey moth as I carry it
between my fingers

to the compost bucket
in the kitchen sink.

With the fine ash
it has left behind

I paint a solitary charcoal stripe
down my arm.

A fire marshal was here earlier:
it's not the law yet,

she told us, but we should
clear the logs stacked below the eaves,

the coyote fence could come out—
the ancient pine latillas,

all their sagas—
taken to the dump. She leaves

a fireproofing plan
with a colorful checklist,

emergency equipment
is suggested: our road

out of the canyon
is narrow.

When the rains do come,
they pond.

Those first few days,
nothing dries up. Dark moisture

suspends like smoke
in clouds above the long spine

of mountainous rock. My shoes
slab with mud as I walk along the ravine.

A piñon root has found
its way into granite

then out
and over

cascading
down the coarse facing

before crawling back
under rock, again

finding soil.
This privacy

a joy I cannot
steal for myself.

First Feel

The dental hygienist runs a slide show of her photographs
of national parks on the monitor above my head, offers me
ear buds and Bach while she gently scrapes
the plaque from my teeth.
The steady removal of excess from a body is satisfying—
but not satisfying enough, anymore.

Someone once asked Sophocles how it feels to get older,
to which he replied, *It feels like I've been released*
by a crazy and mad master.
The mind keeps taunting itself—
aren't you something other than this body?
An hour ago I consumed a *Garden Bear*, 6mg THC,
and am feeling the first waves of relaxation float through my toes,
which are sore because a few small bones in my feet
have begun to crumble.

In the early evening, I walk carefully into the nature conserve,
sit on a wooden bench close to the pond.
Cold mist falls on my open face,
then a faint rainbow above the east mountains.
A heron plucks from the water an infant snapping turtle,
who, stunned in this moment of its death,
stretches fully out of its shell
as if to take a first feel of eternity—
its tiny toenails spread like the points of a star—
as the heron swallows it whole.

Collective Effervescence

It wasn't the lifeless laptop screen
packed with opaque frames or off-tinted faces—
the skittish connections—Zooming in for poetry
class—sometimes just a nose or an eyeball
appearing . . . then vaporizing—all of us so
weary. It wasn't the boxes of salted
piñon caramels my son turned up with,
night after night, the sugar buffering my hips,
or the bottles of Bandol rosé I had introduced
him to, nor his enthusiastic arrival to our patio
most evenings for wine and paprika chicken.
Fearing he might be one of the asymptomatic
he kept his distance so not to kill us. It wasn't
my hungered for, in-person trips to the store,
armed in purple mask with toothy grin,
green rubber gloves, the collective trauma and
strangeness causing all grocery carts to merge
haphazardly in the snack aisle like iron shavings
to magnets, even as we were trying our best
to maneuver away from each other. It wasn't the
kindness of curbside pick-up, the quarts of guacamole,
Oaxacan salsas and soft tortillas carefully
placed in the trunk of my car. It wasn't
even the bristly-coated New Mexico
shepherd, his vocabulary increasing
with the abundance of attention. What it was
was the trees, the forest dense with the thick
puzzly-growth of ponderosa bark, that butterscotch
scent; the limber pines in the courtyard, their
branches leaning in to shade; the nectarine full
of her blushing progeny. What it was was the
black widows, nesting individually yet collectively
in the garden shed so that when I opened the door
their plump abdomens shone like black holes
filling with daylight. What it was is what it is,
the Steller's jays bouncing from mound to mound
of the horse manure we piled around trees in the yard,

white feather markings alongside their beaks like face paint,
their navy crests bounding with effervescence
at discovering seed after seed, worm after worm,
in those decomposing worlds of moist dung.

Given an Invitation

Light spreads out oddly now: winter mornings as the bathroom blinds are raised, I wonder is this early spring, late fall? An unmistakable *snap* of bird crashing into thermal pane. Five in four days. Northern flicker. Steller's jay. Brown nuthatch. Ruby-crowned kinglet. Western bluebird. The tree that grows over the well is weeping. A coyote comes down the hill, stops to chew on one of his legs. Yes, the light is different, but not by much. Someone reports cherry blossoms blooming early December, in Providence. Given an invitation to be hanged, drawn and quartered, the Earth says, *Yes, take me, whatever you need.* I remember this walk: it was years ago. Snow coming down in bulky blankets of fog and me on the road, in heavy boots, a pair of ski poles so as not to slip on the ice. Already a florescent glow from the street lights at 2 pm. In the distance, the mountains had flattened into that kind of white that is blue, and I looked up high through the skeleton of cottonwoods. Huddled in close to the place where a branch meets the trunk were a few small birds who stay the winter. Pressing their wings firm to their bodies, their backs mounded with fresh snow like tops of fence posts—they were singing with fury. A chorale performing for an audience of aspens and pines.

> They were singing
> For the rapture of being
> Covered in snow, in winter

Eye of a Storm

We should all have pockets for our feelings
the way True's beaked whales have pockets for their fins
and can tuck them in for efficient movement during diving.
Each speck of cosmic dust has an eye like a tropical cyclone,
distinctive the way snowflakes have their own fragile patterns,
which feel nearly human to those who gravitate
toward tender melting things.
Most everything feels human
to a human. *Art is about something the way a cat
is about the house*, said Allen Grossman, wise poet
of the personal. His feelings are about us All, the way a street light
in Italy is about a drinking fountain under a tree in Milwaukee.
Nick Cave uses buttons and plastic and faux fur,
says his sculptural work *Is like a second skin that hides gender, race, class.*
All our colors named to explain ourselves to our selves.
My feelings—red in tooth and claw—
for this primate in a tiny glass cage
who has been experimented on, are hanging all over
my mind in tufts and blisters the way the fur,
and the skin underneath the fur, is hanging all over
this creature's body. His penis is raw with open sores.
We see him considering the lens of the camera,
and then the person filming— *Won't you help me?*
And then more videos pop up on my laptop, more
tortured animals, their horns torn off, their abdomens knifed—
insides pulsing—the storming eyes ceaseless, cochineal.

There You Are Again, Melancholy

                              hounding the mind
                unable to decide
                              panic or dread—

a dog buries a bone, digs it up,

buries it again.

          Through the window I watch morning clouds
                                        cover the
                              mounting sun

                and then the sun is exposed
                              shadows emerge, then vanish
          on the ceiling of the bathroom

                              as if a light dimmer is being
                turned up and down.

Isn't memory like this?
          Something concealed is suddenly animated:

                a sunrise, so many years ago—
                        my high school love sat outside the Corner Store
                              on a milk crate,
                              sorting newspapers

when a tow truck jumped the curb—
                it's chain snaking behind the flatbed,

                        hooked him around the waist,

                        then dragged him through the
                              quiet streets
until his teeth fell down his throat,

and his face became unrecognizable.

At the wake,
    the coffin closed,
        I thought of his velvet cheeks,

                                      his precious lips,
                                          that just a few days
before

            had been   pressed to mine,

had passed a softening toffee
into my mouth.

Okjökull

Didn't I tell you what happened to my youngest brother the day before Thanksgiving? Nooo? That's right, we had dinner like two nights before I took off for home, and I guess we haven't talked since. Oh, I just loved that izakaya—didn't we have so much fun? I love sharing food with you, those small bowls of handmade noodles (which you called the sorrow of someone's fingertips), that amazing burdock tempura, and the bottle of chilled sake (which you said was the desire of someone's cognizance). Oh, I just adore you! It was totally stunning how they served the sake to us in a ceramic carafe, the Artic white of an ivory gull. You were so good to listen to all my horrific stories! It was a lot to drop on you at once. All my brothers gone—poof—vanished—in one year. I told you, right? How first my oldest younger brother killed himself at a shooting range, turned the practice gun from the bullseye to his head, a teenage attendant looking on, and that my second youngest brother took his life with pills as malignancy ravaged his chest just a few months later. My shrink says sharing grief with friends helps transform trauma to drama. I know I didn't forget to tell you about my cousin, how he killed his wife and young children. Yup, gunned them while they were playing on the backyard swing set, then went over to his in-laws' house, washed his hands at the kitchen sink, took an egg salad sandwich off the platter, and casually sat down with them to watch a ball game on TV. My shrink says we use the patterns our stories create to try to make sense of our lives. Well, you are not going to believe this. So, the day before Thanksgiving, my youngest brother was jogging in the snow and dropped to the trail. Dead. Instantly. A massive coronary at 38. Can you deal with these genes? His girlfriend was with him. They were deep in the park and the EMT had to go on foot. Of course, there was like nothing they could do. Yes, don't worry, I am seeing my shrink five days a week right now. But wait, I haven't told you what also happened. My brother, the one who shot himself in the head at the shooting range, loved everything Japanese, and for years he studied how to write ideograms. He had my parents' number written on an index card in an outside pocket of his jacket and the attendant, who was 15—way too young to be doing that job, but it was his father who owned the place—he went through the jacket and found the card. The number was printed in block letters, which my brother had colored in with an ice-blue Sharpie. There were also cartoon drawings of cats in various "lifeless" poses, do you know what I mean? And a few lines of Japanese characters. When I was home I called the shooting range to see how the kid was doing, and after I explained who I was, to whomever answered the phone, she said, *Girlfriend, sit down,* then she told me the kid had taken one of the guns from the office after an argument with his father about his curfew, went behind the building and shot himself in the jugular. His head phones on. His iPod set to repeat that vile song, *Ok Boomer.* Have you ever heard it? But let's not talk about this now. How are you doing? How is your insanely gorgeous guy? Did you read about the glacier that just like vanished in Iceland? I mean, it didn't just vanish—it had been on its way out for years. They were watching it like it was a woman pregnant with identical octuplets. But really, a funeral for a glacier? Are we not so preposterously melodramatic about our catastrophes?

乾杯
かんぱい

Negativity Bias

We are wired
to expect things will go wrong—
and when they do, to remember them
more vividly than all the beautiful fragments of our lives.

We pretend that worry might predict an outcome.
I place my hands evenly on the table
fan the phalanges,
listen to the whirl of a buzz saw cutting through planks

in the neighbor's driveway below.
I seek evidence to confirm what I believe—
who would expect wild chickens on a Florida cay
or that while I was looking one way

a leashed dog would leap across the sidewalk and sink its teeth
into my daughter's thigh?
From what I imagine, the sea will continue its ascent,
still I want, so badly, to hold things in place.

I walk past a man on Elizabeth Street
wearing a FUCK LETTUCE tee-shirt,
the U an applique of a ribeye—
someone went to a lot of trouble to get this just so—
to fit the steak into place like the slats of a veranda.

Earlier there was the buoyant chatter of wild chickens
mating under the creaking eaves of tin roofs,
rainwater from the gutters rolling off their backs.
Like worry, chickens pluck and pluck at indigestibles.

I squeeze my right wrist with my left hand,
the ulna pops—
a sharp ache hurries into my upper trapezius.
This is the evidence I am looking for.

Fire Ants

A rattlesnake is a hallucination— chartreuse on black—
departs its shed skin under the exhausted

Jonathan apple while I twist
in sleep. Up-mountain

seven acres blaze into seven hundred,
then seven thousand. My slender fingers

curl into palms, wrists bend toward sky—
I make my pillows wet.

My thighs are burning. How many legs
on how many spiders

are crisped to an absent stench?
Forget about escape. Forget about

not being able to see what I descry.
At an outdoor market

a pile of deep fried ants fills a turquoise bowl.
Toothpicks stacked for sampling.

The art of death
is not an art of adaptation,

it is an art of reinvention.
A smoke forest becomes the cloud forest

where I once watched the cumulus atop mountains
turn into goddesses clothed in satin,

watched them leap until they were naked,
their golden bangles slipping one by one

out of the ether,
ringing the rocky peaks.

Allegory with Fiestaware

For a few moments there wasn't anything else
      but an evening grosbeak pressed under claws
                  to a branch of the nectarine tree
as the young Cooper's hawk tore through the feathers
            and flicked them
                        into the air.

      The raptor jerked his head one way, then the other,
with each tug and swallow of the sinewy flesh.
              His red eye a waning sun.

It wasn't long until the other birds that had darted away
      congregated again at the feeder.

A cluster of lesser finches around the orange Fiestaware plate
      on a birdbath stand, piled with thistle and black-oil
           sunflower seeds.

The hawk had flown in rearward,
           scooping his wings
back and up as if trying to stay afloat in water
           his legs thrust out in front—
talons spearing the fleeing bird like an hors d'oeuvre.

      The yearling scours the bark for any speck of
remaining flesh,
        shakes his head and hops
to another branch, begins to groom his plumage,
    then seeing me in the window,
        soars away.

Beneath the tree, feathers cover the crowns
    of full-seeded dandelion heads,
        are caught in crevices of bark,
            nestle atop the river rock wall.

But the bones, the eyes, the feet, the beak,
    the rest of the evening grosbeak

        is nightfall.

The Pine Forest Is My Home

Watercress grows on the banks of the stream
and the woods race wild with small-budded red columbine—
Indian paintbrush splashed everywhere, shadowing
the lankiness of daisies. I feel so close to the hundreds
of caterpillars that stand upright on tall blades of grass.
They sway back and forth with the wind as if in supplication
to the sky. Hear them drop off—then listen—they slide back
to the same stalk of grass. When I block the way
with my finger, a caterpillar raises its head, turns
in the opposite direction, then twists back toward its altar.

Young Sophie whose name is carved deeply
into the wide trunk of an ancient aspen was in love
with Sebastiano and probably not thinking *Someday*
a monarch caterpillar will nestle inside the tail
of this **S**—cocoon itself the way her body body-hugged
Sebastiano all night and into the next day in the canvas
pup tent they had set up under the Blackjack canopy
near a mountain creek, where today, maybe sixty years later,
soaking my tired feet in the cold water,
I rescue a wiggling caterpillar before it drowns,

                    while at the same time
                    on a raft made of pine bark
                    another floats by

An Exultation of Spirit

I wish I could say that a surgeon's knife
in the small of my back and the successful removal
of some extra bone, the liberation of a cornered nerve,
would be enough to jump start me back into the joy of living,
and that this morning—as I watched a massive raven,
much larger than I would have thought,
land on the rim of the birdbath and drop a mouse carcass in,
hop away, pick it back up with its beak, drop it in again,
shake it around in the water, gulp a few sips, then fly off
with the baptized meal—I wish I could say that it was enough,
to have observed this clever raven—to see that its practice
was wise, and after, when I went out to make fresh again
the water for the other birds and found the entrails, the stomach,
a bloated liver, floating in the shallow water, I wish I could say
that I felt grateful for my life—
to be present in the raw early morning,
in this orchard of aspens and wild plums—the damp pines
bending their boughs toward my house, but what I received
was not an exultation of spirit, but rather a yank in the flesh,
much like a set of new stitches being ripped out—blessed is not
what you receive in this life, blessed is how you renounce it.

Very Long Marriage at Bedtime

I had somehow not remembered
that any number times zero is zero.
David said, think of it this way,
20 zeros are nothing. We were in bed,
teeth cleaned, night guards ready
on the bedside tables. His three pillows
stacked behind his head, my five arranged like a boat
to cradle my back, an almost orange
moon penetrating our window through
smoky darkness like a blaze about to leap
across an expanse of pine forest. How
did this happen? All these years together
compressed into this moment of repeating
moments, so many of them indistinguishable,
so few of them recallable. What does dividing
any number by zero do to that number?
This is sort of fascinating, he says, that you
don't remember any of this. He rolls
toward me, glides his hands around my hips.
His breath is minty, the skin on his face, flushed.
You're cute, he says, what else
don't you remember?
I remember running into you
at the Albuquerque airport, honey,
I say, after not seeing you for so many years.
You wore black jeans and a black tee shirt,
a black belt with a sliver buckle, black
Dr. Martens; I looked at you, your jet-black hair,
and somehow I saw that we were about to combine
sorrows and joys into the terrifying equation
of two people equaling one home. I remember
being panicked, my heart leaping into an abyss,
then sinking to my stomach as I watched
what was to become the rest of my life
glide his luggage off the carrousel. I remember
every minute of each labor, each delivery
for both children, and how going into the birthing

room for the second time, I remembered:
pay attention as the baby exits, that final
wet sliding out of me. I remembered
to pause for one of the swiftest moments
in my life, a whole new warm body
joining the living.

Acknowledgments

Enormous gratitude to the editors of the following publications where these poems first appeared or were reprinted.

About Place Journal: Bleeding Slowly to Death, Eye of a Storm, Mother's Day with Birdbath and Wildfires

Academy of American Poets Poem-a-Day: Quantum Foam

American Poetry Review: The Story of Her Arrival, No House, Love, I Am

Chameleon Chimera, an Anthology of South Florida Poets, Purple Ink Press: Quantum Foam

Cutthroat: One Taste, The Pine Forest Is My Home

Dark Land Sky: produced Shooting Star and Bolide as a special podcast and will present the poem as a broadside in their ongoing exhibition series beginning with Bone Springs Art Space in Roswell, New Mexico.

El Palacio, the Magazine of the Museum of New Mexico commissioned Moonrise over Hernandez and this poem was also made into a letter press broadside by master printer Tom Leech from the New Mexico History Museum

Ginko Prize: There Are as Many Songs in the World as Branches of Coral received an award and was published in the 2020 *Ecopoetry Anthology*

Hole in the Head Review: Hour of Lead (reprinted), Okjökull

Lana Turner: Hour of Lead, Shooting Star and Bolide

Los Angeles Review: Very Long Marriage with Lacerations

New Mexico Poetry Anthology, edited by state poet laureate Levi Romero and Michelle Ortega: The Sweetness off Each Other's Bodies, Given an Invitation

On The Seawall: Coronae, Fire Ants, An Exultation of Spirit, Collective Effervescence, Very Long Marriage at Bedtime, Not One; Not Two, Negativity Bias

Plume: Notes on Desire, Three Stages of Friendship and Grief

Poetry Daily: Love, I Am, reprinted as a feature poem

Rise Up Review: *I Don't See Anything at the End of It*

SoFloPoJo: The Day after My 27-Year-Old Daughter Was Not Incinerated in an Apartment Full of Natural Gas, I Roam and Recollect

SWWIM: For Whom Do You Bathe and Make Yourself Beautiful?

The Ecopoetry Anthology: Volume II (forthcoming from Trinity University Press in 2025), There Are as Many Songs in the World as Branches of Coral

Terrain.org: Allegory with Fiestaware

The Nature of Our Times: Ephemera, Hour of Lead (reprint), Mother's Day with Birdbath and Wildfires (reprinted)

Vox Populi: There Are as Many Songs in the World as Branches of Coral (reprinted), Love, I Am (reprinted)

Zocalo Public Square: Canyon Road

A Brown Stone was published as a chapbook by dancing girl press

It is with immeasurable gratitude that I offer much appreciation to Free Verse Editions series editor Jon Thompson and Parlor Press publisher Dave Blakesley for their generosity, for publishing this book and for all the exquisite work they do. Friends who have, over the years, offered insights on these poems, I am in deep admiration of your own work, and I thank you: Chase Twichell, Sawnie Morris, Anne Marie Macari, Malena Morling, Miriam Sagan, Carol Moldaw, Jenny George, Tyler Mills, Victoria Redel, Michael Hettich, Arne Weingart, Elena Karina Byrne, Pamela Uschuk and Tony Hoagland—in remembrance—had his eyes on many of these poems. I am grateful to Santa Fe's Center for Contemporary Arts (CCA), where for many years I have been curating the Community Reading Series, organizing workshops for other poets and teaching my own workshops, and to the Witter Bynner Foundation for Poetry—my community work has received nine consecutive grants since 2015, funding projects including WingSpan, Poetry Pollinators and my work at CCA. I would also like to thank the Academy of American Poets for a generous 2020 Poets Laureate Fellowship, The Morton Marcus Poetry Prize, especially Donna Mekis and Brad Crenshaw, for selecting my poem "One Taste" for this 2024 award, and East Hill for an exceptional summer residency. To my family: David Kaufman—first reader, last reader and everything in between, Willa Kaufman, Oliver Kaufman, and David Modigliani, I offer my gratitude and innumerable future meals.

A very special thank you to artist Alexandra Eldridge (alexandraeldridge.com) for her kindness and support and for permission to use her photo-based painting "Sea Goddess" as the cover image for this book.

Dedications

"Three Stages of Friendship and Grief" is for Tony Hoagland.

"Okjökull" is for one of my dearest friends, with huge love and admiration.

Notes

The Chan koan, "Each branch of coral holds up the moon" is reimagined for the title of this collection and is from Baling Haojian's 巴陵顥鑑 (Pa-ling Hao-chien, Haryo Kokan) Three Barriers: A person of the way asked, "What is the blown-feather sword that cuts away delusion?" Baling responded, "Each branch of coral holds up the moon." Case 100, The Blue Cliff Record.

In this morning's sunshine an illuminated face sings is translated from the Japanese by Joan Sutherland, and is from her book *Acequias & Gates*.

"Love, I Am" references Baling's "Snow in a Silver Bowl," Case 13, The Blue Cliff Record, and was inspired by and uses one line from Robert Creeley's poem "The Rain."

"Not One; Not Two" is inspired by the Vimalakirti Sutra, an ancient Mahāyāna Buddhist text.

"For Whom Do You Bathe and Make Yourself Beautiful?" is a Zen koan from Dongshan's Five Ranks, second cycle.

The title of the poem *Hour of Lead* is taken from the third stanza of Emily Dickinson's poem *After great pain, a formal feeling comes –* (372)

I Don't See Anything at the End of It is Larry Levis's line from *Boy in Video Arcade.*

In *There Are as Many Songs in the World as Branches of Coral* the word starfish is used to be consistent with the past. Now this creature is more accurately called a sea star.

Okjökull is the name of a former glacier in Iceland, the first one to disappear. A plaque in Icelandic and English, was installed where it once was and reads:

A letter to the future

Ok is the first Icelandic glacier to lose its status as a glacier. In the next 200 years all our glaciers are expected to follow the same path. This monument is to acknowledge that we know what is happening and what needs to be done. Only you know if we did it.

"Ok Boomer" is a song by Peter Kuli.

乾杯　かんぱい (Kanpai!) means *dry cup* or *Cheers!* in Japanese.

The Pine Forest Is My Home uses two lines from Hanshan, translated by Kazuaki Tanahashi and Peter Levitt.

About the Author

Elizabeth Jacobson was the fifth Poet Laureate of Santa Fe, New Mexico and an Academy of American Poets Laureate Fellow. Her second collection of poems, *Not into the Blossoms and Not into the Air*, won the New Measure Poetry Prize, selected by Marianne Boruch (Free Verse Editions/Parlor Press, 2019) and the 2019 New Mexico-Arizona Book Award for both New Mexico Poetry and Best New Mexico Book. Her other books include *Her Knees Pulled In* (Tres Chicas Books, 2012), two chapbooks from dancing girl press and *Everything Feels Recent When You're Far Away: Poetry and Art from Santa Fe Youth During the Pandemic* (Axle Books, 2021), which she co-edited. Her poems have been published in many literary journals including the *American Poetry Review, Lana Turner, On The Seawall, Plume*, the *Los Angeles Review*, and her community projects have received nine consecutive grants from the Witter Bynner Foundation for Poetry. Elizabeth is a reviews editor for the on-line literary magazine *Terrain.org*, and she directs the poetry programs at Santa Fe's Center for Contemporary Arts (CCA).

Please visit https://linktr.ee/ElizabethJacobson

Photograph of the author by Kevin Guevara.
Used by permission.

Free Verse Editions

Edited by Jon Thompson

13 ways of happily by Emily Carr
& in Open, Marvel by Felicia Zamora
& there's you still thrill hour of the world to love by Aby Kaupang
Alias by Eric Pankey
the atmosphere is not a perfume it is odorless by Matthew Cooperman
At Your Feet (A Teus Pés) by Ana Cristina César, edited by
    Katrina Dodson, trans. by Brenda Hillman and Helen Hillman
Bari's Love Song by Kang Eun-Gyo, translated by Chung Eun-Gwi
Between the Twilight and the Sky by Jennie Neighbors
Blade Work by Lily Brown
Blood Orbits by Ger Killeen
The Bodies by Christopher Sindt
The Book of Isaac by Aidan Semmens
The Calling by Bruce Bond
Canticle of the Night Path by Jennifer Atkinson
Child in the Road by Cindy Savett
Civil Twilight by Giles Goodland
Condominium of the Flesh by Valerio Magrelli, trans. by Clarissa Botsford
Contrapuntal by Christopher Kondrich
Country Album by James Capozzi
Cry Baby Mystic by Daniel Tiffany
The Curiosities by Brittany Perham
Current by Lisa Fishman
Day In, Day Out by Simon Smith
Dear Reader by Bruce Bond
Dismantling the Angel by Eric Pankey
Divination Machine by F. Daniel Rzicznek
Elsewhere, That Small by Monica Berlin
Empire by Tracy Zeman
Erros by Morgan Lucas Schuldt
Extinction of the Holy City by Bronisław Maj, trans. by Daniel Bourne
Fifteen Seconds without Sorrow by Shim Bo-Seon, trans. by
    Chung Eun-Gwi and Brother Anthony of Taizé
The Forever Notes by Ethel Rackin
The Flying House by Dawn-Michelle Baude
General Release from the Beginning of the World by Donna Spruijt-Metz
Ghost Letters by Baba Badji

Go On by Ethel Rackin
Here City by Rick Snyder
I Am Not Korean by Song Kyeong-dong
An Image Not a Book by Kylan Rice
Instances: Selected Poems by Jeongrye Choi, trans. by Brenda Hillman,
    Wayne de Fremery, & Jeongrye Choi
Invitatory by Molly Spencer
Last Morning by Simon Smith
The Magnetic Brackets by Jesús Losada, trans. by M. Smith & L. Ingelmo
Man Praying by Donald Platt
A Map of Faring by Peter Riley
The Miraculous Courageous by Josh Booton
Mirrorforms by Peter Kline
M O 月 N by Chengru He
A Myth of Ariadne by Martha Ronk
No Shape Bends the River So Long by Monica Berlin & Beth Marzoni
North | Rock | Edge by Susan Tichy
Not into the Blossoms and Not into the Air by Elizabeth Jacobson
Overyellow, by Nicolas Pesquès, translated by Cole Swensen
Parallel Resting Places by Laura Wetherington
pH of Au by Vanessa Couto Johnson
Physis by Nicolas Pesquès, translated by Cole Swensen
Pilgrimage Suites by Derek Gromadzki
Pilgrimly by Siobhán Scarry
Poems from above the Hill & Selected Work by Ashur Etwebi, trans. by
    Brenda Hillman & Diallah Haidar
The Prison Poems by Miguel Hernández, trans. by Michael Smith
Puppet Wardrobe by Daniel Tiffany
Quarry by Carolyn Guinzio
remanence by Boyer Rickel
Republic of Song by Kelvin Corcoran
Rumor by Elizabeth Robinson
Saint with a Peacock Voice by L. S. Klatt
Settlers by F. Daniel Rzicznek
A Short History of Anger by Joy Manesiotis
Signs Following by Ger Killeen
Small Sillion by Joshua McKinney
Split the Crow by Sarah Sousa
Spine by Carolyn Guinzio
Spool by Matthew Cooperman
Strange Antlers by Richard Jarrette

A Suit of Paper Feathers by Nate Duke
Summoned by Guillevic, trans. by Monique Chefdor & Stella Harvey
Sunshine Wound by L. S. Klatt
System and Population by Christopher Sindt
There Are as Many Songs in the World as Branches of Coral by
    Elizabeth Jacobson
These Beautiful Limits by Thomas Lisk
They Who Saw the Deep by Geraldine Monk
The Thinking Eye by Jennifer Atkinson
This History That Just Happened by Hannah Craig
An Unchanging Blue: Selected Poems 1962–1975 by
    Rolf Dieter Brinkmann, trans. by Mark Terrill
Under the Quick by Molly Bendall
Verge by Morgan Lucas Schuldt
The Visible Woman by Allison Funk
The Wash by Adam Clay
Well by Sasha Steensen
We'll See by Georges Godeau, trans. by Kathleen McGookey
What Stillness Illuminated by Yermiyahu Ahron Taub
Winter Journey [Viaggio d'inverno] by Attilio Bertolucci, trans. by
    Nicholas Benson
Wonder Rooms by Allison Funk

www.ingramcontent.com/pod-product-compliance
Lightning Source LLC
Chambersburg PA
CBHW022034090426
42741CB00007B/1054